The Chilling, True Terror of the Black-Eyed Kids

Second Edition

Edited by

G. Michael Vasey

Note – This is a compilation of The Black-Eyed Kids

Your Haunted Lives 3

And the Black-eyed demons are coming

With some new and supplemental material

Copyright ©2017 Asteroth's Books

ISBN - 978-0-9961972-8-1

Table of Contents

Introduction

This book is actually two books in one. In the second edition, I have tried to remove any repetition between the two.

The first book is an investigation of the BEK that also uses encounter stories to illustrate it. The stories are not edited except for readability. The second book is a further collection of encounter stories – again these stories are not edited except for readability.

The conclusions that I present are my own. For me, the BEK stories are perhaps the most chilling and terrifying that have ever been shared with me and even last night as I was editing this book and listening to a radio interview I gave recently, I had the chills. At 3:10am, I was awakened by a knocking sound and I must admit to laying paralyzed with fear for several minutes before daring to roll over and try to sleep again.

If you encounter the BEK, do let me know – I am keen to read all encounter stories and can be contacted at garymvasey at gmail dot com or via the myhauntedlifetoo.com website.

November 2018

G. Michael Vasey

Book One - Introduction

It all began innocently enough. A reader submitted a story to my true ghost stories website at My Haunted Life Too about an encounter with Black-Eyed Children. I read their story with a growing sense of unease and horror. There isn't much that scares me these days, but this story had me thinking about being alone at night and hearing *that* knock at *my* door. I was tingling with a nauseating mixture of fear and fascination reading the submission. I had heard about Black-Eyed Kids, or BEK for short, of course. It was an urban myth, I thought, and one that seemed to be distinctly American in origin.

I posted the story and traffic to the website grew tenfold overnight. It seems I wasn't the only one creeped out by the story as it went viral on social media; shared and shared again. Then, story after story started to flood in about BEK and Black-Eyed People. Many of these encounters seemed to follow a well-worn and similar format to the first submission.

Here is that first submission.

> *A few months ago, I visited my mother in Amarillo. She lives in a nice area that has a good reputation. I was expecting to have a nice vacation and spend some quality time with her, as she is getting older. We spent the afternoon together and that evening, she went to bed. I wasn't tired, so I decided to watch some TV, and catch up with my friends on Facebook. About an hour later there was a knock on the door. I was a little taken aback as this area was normally dead after ten.*
>
> *I went into the kitchen to try and look out to see who was at the door. The knocking was persistent. It wasn't like the average elder visit where a knock would be followed by silence. This was a constant tap-tap-tap.*

I was starting to get tired of this idiot knocking on the door, so I went to the porch and opened the door. Two teenagers stood there. One looked around fourteen, the other around sixteen. I instantly wondered if they were at the wrong house as I was the only person under thirty in my family. There was no possible reason for these kids to be here.

They said nothing, so I asked them what they wanted. The older one told me that he was sorry for waking me up but wanted to come in and use the phone. He explained that they had been left in the area by their parents and needed to call someone. As he finished speaking, he just stared at me. When I saw his eyes, I couldn't tear myself away. They were completely black. Just black. I couldn't break away from his gaze. I had a huge urge to just stand back and let them in. As we stood there staring at each other he started talking again. This time he wasn't asking. He was demanding that I let him in. The façade was gone. Whatever he wanted would only "take a few moments" and then they would leave. He wanted me to "let him in and help him."

I broke my eyes away and realized that I was actually stepping backwards. I hurriedly told them to get off the porch and find help elsewhere. I closed the door with them still standing there and heading towards the phone. I called the police and told them that there were a couple of kids in the area who seemed to be up to no good. They told me later that they did a thorough check—but didn't find anything. No one else in the area had seen them either. My mother hadn't even heard them or the knocking. When I told her about it, she just dismissed it as the youth of today with poor manners.

She didn't see their eyes. I felt absolutely terrified and I felt at odds with their will. I think they meant to do me harm. Has anyone else had any experience with black-eyed kids?

Submitted by Deana M

That was the first story that awakened me to this strange phenomenon known as the Black-Eyed Kids or BEK and with my curiosity piqued; I had to find out more. What were these young kids with black eyes doing knocking on people's doors and terrorizing communities with their strange activities?

The first thing to note is that all of the encounters largely follow the same predictable pattern or format as follows. Late at night, there is a knock at the door. When the door is answered, there are one or more – usually two, young kids, in their early teens. For some reason, the person opening the door is immediately gripped with an insane fear that seems to originate at the very core of their being or soul. Their heart pounds and they want to run and escape but seemingly are unable, and they are instead, rooted to the spot. The kids aren't usually threatening or violent, but are rather devoid of any emotion and quietly but insistently demand to be let in. The reasons they give to enter vary from using the phone to wanting something to eat or drink. It is usually at some time around this point in the story that the person notices the kid's eyes and is even more horrified by what they see. The eyes are totally black. There is no white, no iris, and just total pools of blackness. This is often the catalyst for them to slam the door shut and wait inside the house until they are certain the kids have left. Sometimes, despite the horror and intense urge to run, the idea of a young teen out alone at night brings out the better side in the door answerer who, at least for a while, contemplates helping them. In almost all cases, the intense fear eventually makes them close the door and cower behind it, sometimes even calling the police.

The story is repeated over and over by the many people who have shared their creepy encounters, with only minor changes in the detail. Sometimes, no one else sees or hears the kids, as in the encounter above. Sometimes, they leave no visible footsteps in the snow or wet. Although they are physical kids, they seem capable of vanishing and of being notice only by their intended victim. Sometimes adult Black-Eyed People are also involved in the periphery of the story as if waiting for the kids to gain entry or they pick up the kids later.

Here is another example of a story we published on the website.

I recently read with interest your story about two Black Eyed kids who tried to gain entry to a ladies' house. I too had an experience with a Black-Eyed person.

I took my family on vacation last year. We stayed at a motel near Lake Country, California. It's a nice area with plenty of things for the kids to do. Everything had been going well, and we had been having a lot of fun.

On our fourth night, we were in our room watching TV, when someone knocked on the door. We weren't expecting any visitors, so I elected to simply ignore it. The knocking continued and whatever was on the other side of the door started growling. I shouted out and told them that they had the wrong room, and that we weren't expecting anyone. The knocking ceased. A few moments later it started again, and a voice started shouting, "Let me in." It was a female voice, but devoid of any emotion. Then we started to hear the same thing happening up and down all along the corridor. Multiple voices all screaming, "let me in." We were terrified at this point wondering just what was going on.

I got up and looked out of the window. Two people were walking into the building. Both looked normal until one of them noticed that I was standing at the window. I saw her eyes. They were completely black. In every other sense, she looked normal. But I am sure both the girl who saw me, and the man she was with were Black Eyed people.

When the commotion finally died down, I ventured out of our room and went over to the reception block. The receptionist told me that she had received no complaints, and that she had been on duty the whole time. She had no explanation for what I was telling her. I think she actually thought I was insane. I just wonder what would have happened if I had opened the door? Would I be here to tell this story? We won't be going to Lake County again, I can tell you that.

Submitted by Rick R

Here is yet another encounter.

This incident happened to me around five years ago. It was in December, or January and we were having particularly strong snowstorms at the time.

I had been in bed for a few hours when I started to hear tapping noises coming from several windows in my house. It must have been around 3am. I just thought it was some kids in the neighborhood making Asses of themselves. So, I got up, went downstairs and opened the door. Two boys were standing there. Now, remember this is the middle of winter and these two boys are standing there in thin jackets and pants. The cold didn't seem to bother them one bit. I also started to feel very anxious — scared even. I couldn't explain it at the time.

The smaller of the boys suddenly started talking. He had a monotone voice, with absolutely no emotion of any kind. He asked if he could use the "telegraph." Now... I was expecting him to want to use the phone, or perhaps the bathroom... but the telegraph?

At the same time, I noticed that the whole neighborhood had become deathly quiet. No dogs barking, no humming of wires, no cars... nothing.

I told the two boys that I didn't have a telegraph in my house and asked them to go home and reconsider their lives. I also explained that playing fool and asking for a telegraph was a dumb thing to be doing at such an early hour with a grumpy old man like myself.

They didn't even flinch. I closed the door and the tapping on the windows started again. I felt absolutely drained. That's when they started screaming and shouting for me to let them in. I grabbed the phone in my hall and dialed for the police. The screams and shouts should have been audible over the phone — but the lady who took my call didn't seem to hear them. She said that they would send a patrol car. Later I was told that she hadn't taken my call seriously, and no patrol car had been dispatched.

I went back upstairs as the tapping and banging continued. I eventually fell asleep and haven't seen these kids since. But I do want to know what the hell was going on. I haven't been able to get the whole thing out of my mind. What did they want with the telegraph?

Submitted by Roy D.

Apparently, these BEK cannot only disappear at will but can also appear in highly unusual places finding high-level security no barrier at all.

I'm in the USAF and I live on base. I had never encountered anything strange on base until this particular incident happened. I was on base one weekend. Almost everyone else was home, drinking, sleeping or on duty. I had only stayed that weekend because I'd spent all my money.

I was on my bunk watching a movie when I heard a knock at my door. I thought it was my roommate. I went and opened it. Instead of a roommate, I found two kids standing on the walkway – only these kids freaked the hell out of me. I don't know what it was about them, but we're always told to listen to what's inside, because it just might save your life. Right then that voice was screaming at me to shut the door and lock those kids out.

There was also the little telltale sign that these kids had pitch-black eyes. I mean there was absolutely

*no white or any other color to them whatsoever –
just pure black. I asked them what they were
doing here at this time of night. One of them told
me that it was cold out, and that they wanted to
come in and read. I had never met a kid that
wanted to "come in and read," and I knew for a
fact that they didn't belong on this base. They
didn't mention any parents, any broken-down cars
or even how they had managed to get this far out
to the base. There was nothing sincere about these
kids. They were playing a game.*

*It was at this point when I noticed that I could not
drag my eyes away from theirs. I felt like I was
being sucked in. It felt absolutely horrendous – as
though my life were being dragged from my body
screaming. They just stood there with their mouths
closed, eyes staring into mine and no emotion at
all.*

*I prayed for someone else to come by – but nobody
did. I glanced around, the kids stepped forward,
and I stepped back and slammed the door shut. I
felt as though I were in grave danger. Every
warning bell was going off in my head. I stepped
back and fell on my bunk. Drained of energy.*

*I heard soft knocking against the door for a few
minutes, shuffling feet and then nothing. The next
morning, I went down and asked one of the officers
on duty if he had seen the kids. He hadn't. Reading
the accounts on your site, I believe I came face to
face with these kids on a military base. How did
they get in? I have no idea? Where did they go? I
have no idea – but if they can get onto a military
campus – they can get anywhere.*

Sifting through these alarming accounts, a couple of other things should be noticed. It is as if only the person answering the door sees these kids. No one else seems to see them, nor even hear them, even when they are making quite a racket knocking on doors or asking to be let in! Notice also the feeling of being drained of energy – it is as if these kids are energy vampires as well. In fact, as stated above, these encounters mostly all have several common sinister features –a formula if you will, to them that we will explore in more detail below.

The BEK Storyline

The BEK don't seem to often threaten. They don't shout angrily or resort to physical violence it seems. They don't seem to need to. They just stand there, emotionless beings talking in a quiet, almost hypnotic, voice first asking and then later, demanding entry. This combination of the monotonous calm voice repeating their request and the dark pools of black that are their eyes, seemingly combine to hypnotize and lull the person answering the door, despite the fear that they feel at the very core of their being. They know or believe themselves to be in mortal danger and yet they afford the BEK every opportunity to compel them to let them in. Even when armed, the door opener still makes the mistake of opening the door and despite every fiber in their body telling them to point the gun, they lower the weapon.

I have my own experience of these "black-eyed kids." It happened a few years ago. I have never been able to really think of a rational reason for what happened. It just happened.

I headed out to mow my lawn. In the front of the ditch of my road, I have bushes and flowers neatly set up. To my bitter surprise, someone had gone by and stepped all over my roses. I was pretty upset.

The next day, I saw two kids walking down my road. Keep in mind my road has several houses, so we all know each other very well. These kids looked to be around fourteen, or fifteen years old. I've never seen these kids before in the neighborhood. I wanted to go outside and ask them if they messed with my roses, but I figured they're just kids and I'd let it slide this time.

The kids stopped walking and just stood on the road right across from my house. That's a good hundred, or so, feet away. They just stood there. I was looking out the window and they were just standing right there. I went to my room to go get my shoes and when I came out, they were gone.

It was around 8 p.m. and it was starting to get dark out. My power went off and on a few times. That's never happened before. We usually have very stable electricity. Around 8:20, I heard deep knocking at my front door. I went over to the door, turned on my porch light and looked through the little hole on my door, but it was just pitch black, even though the light was on. I didn't know why, but I was extremely terrified. I started to put my hand on the handle and I asked, "Who's there?"

Some kid answered, "Sorry to bother you, but we are lost and need to borrow your phone."

"I have a spare cell phone you can borrow for a few minutes," I told them. "Let me go get it and I'll come outside with you."

The kid just said, "No. You let me in right now!" And he started banging on my door. I'm not talking about just hitting it, but it was like something very big and wide was smashing against my door.

I said, "You quit that right now. I got a gun, and if you try anything, I will shoot you."

The kid kept screaming, "Let me in now! You're making a mistake!"

I grabbed my gun and held it off to the side of my leg. I put my hand on the lock and unlocked the door. This is where I made my mistake. I opened the door expecting either those kids or just one kid with a weapon or something. But these weren't little kids. Standing at my door were two people, and both looked young. But their eyes gave them away. They were pitch black.

I felt terrified again. I felt like putting my shotgun down and letting them in. I'm not sure why I felt that way. As I had the door open for those 3 or 4 seconds, the taller kid started to walk forward to come in. I kicked my door shut as hard as I could, and I locked it.

At this point I heard them both crying and screaming in a strange distorted high-pitched way, followed by some banging on my door again. I went to check my back door, just to make sure it was still locked. Thankfully, my back door was locked and by the time I headed to my front door, they just stopped.

I loaded my shotgun and opened the door expecting these "things". But they were gone. I heard some footsteps and my neighbor was coming by. He heard some weird screams and came by to check on me. I stood there, probably looking like death with a shotgun in my hand. I let him in and told him the entire event. He told me to call the cops, but I was positive they wouldn't believe me. I never called the cops.

Submitted by Keith W.

In that story, there were a couple of additional and noteworthy embellishments to the common storyline. Firstly, the kids appeared in daylight hours and stood over the road ominously looking into the house. This too is a common theme in many BEK experiences, as we will see. It adds to the fear level and the overall strangeness of the experience. The second is the strange high-pitched screaming noises that they made, but this too is echoed by other experiences of this strange phenomenon. Finally, his power went off and on unusually. This is often a feature of the storyline.

> *I have seen these children usually in groups of two late at night roaming around the historic Rte. 66 or 6th street. They seem to pick certain houses as I was told by an older lady who lives alone, they had knocked on her door and said they had been left behind and needed to use the phone. She wouldn't let them in. They seemed mad, but she shut the door and didn't answer again.*

Submitted by Tammy P.

Here is another one from a lady in Odessa.

> *One evening I was sitting in my bedroom reading a book. It must have been around 1am and was a Friday night. My husband worked nights, so I usually tried to stay up for him. I heard a knocking. It wasn't a normal knock; it was a slow, constant one. I got up out of bed to see what it was. I looked out of the window and to my surprise*

saw two young children. I opened the window and asked them what they wanted at this time of night. They replied by saying a simply, "Let us in."

Now I didn't recognize these children at all – they weren't the kids from next door. They were dressed in black clothes and looked dirty. I did wonder if they were runaways, and it did cross my mind to call the Sheriff. I said no and asked what for and all I got back from them was, "We want to use your bathroom." I was quite shocked that children of about I'd say 10 years old wanted to use a stranger's bathroom at this time of night. So, I told them no. I closed the window, but looked at them through the glass, and to my surprise I glanced at their eyes and I have never ever seen eyes like them. They were black, completely black. I got the feeling of evil and unhappiness. It surrounded me. It was horrible.

The knocking continued for two hours. A slow but rhythmic knocking that reached all around the house. I picked up the phone several times – but the phone line was dead. I didn't dare look outside again. When my husband arrived home, he said that he didn't see anything outside, I told him about the phone and he checked it. It was live. I haven't seen the kids since.

Once again, in this encounter, only the lady seemed to see the BEK and electrical items were disturbed, in this case, it was the phone.

Now, not all the stories are about kids. As stated above, Black-Eyed Adults are sometimes seen as well, and it seems that in some instances, these Black-Eyed Adults also try to get a ride, gain entry or get you to give them permission to do something. Here are a couple of examples.

I am a grocery store employee in Idaho. I work in the electronics department, and I have a deep interest in the paranormal. A few weeks ago, now, I was on the floor just making sure everything was correctly shelved. I was walking around, and I had noticed this man come around completely by himself. He was wearing regular clothes, nothing unusual about him really, so I continued on with what I was doing. He just kept walking around my department and kept looking around the store, like he was lost or something. One thing I noticed that was weird about him was the way he walked. He didn't walk with a normal stride, but in a way, it was almost like a slow-motion type walk, yet not as dramatic and obvious as you would picture such a walk. It's hard to explain, but it was just a weird, slow walk.

After noticing that, I continued to work. I had bent down to pick up some trash on the floor, and when I stood back up, he was a good 10 feet away, and he was staring straight at me. Completely motionless, we stood looking at each other. All of a sudden, his eyes turned completely black, no white parts or iris or anything -- just completely black -- but it only happened for a couple of seconds, just long enough for me to realize he was "different".

I made a puzzled face and broke eye contact with him and continued working, and he just went away. I don't know if he was a demon or what, but I do know it puzzled me and still does. After reading your Black-Eyed kid accounts I wonder if he was one of them?

Submitted by Roger M.

A few weeks ago, this happened to me. I saw a story from your site on Facebook and felt that I should share my experience. It wasn't as dramatic as some of the ones I've read, but it was strange.

I was shopping in a mall with my dad, north of San Diego. Across from the car park there was a person talking to himself. He didn't have a phone and there was nobody else he could have possibly been talking to. Dad went ahead into the mall and I headed over to a convenience store to get some cigarettes. I had to go past the strange man. I walked past him, and he said he could not drive on any highway with the number 10 on it and he had to go in the direction of Los Angeles. I said that I couldn't take him. He said that I had to take him to Los Angeles. This was all strange, as he would have to go on I-5 to get to LA.

This was in the middle of the afternoon on a bright and sunny day. His eyes were coal black with no whites in them. He didn't show any emotion and spoke with a monotone voice that really did stand out in this area. His face looked almost dead in appearance. At the time, I thought he must have been some kind-of drug addict. But I wasn't scared; there are a lot of drug addicts in Los Angeles.

He told me that he wanted me to drive him to Los

Angeles and would pay me 'good' money. I told him no. He kept staring at me; I ignored him and walked into the store. As I paid for my cigarettes the man walked around the corner and I didn't see him again. He didn't show any emotion. He wasn't angry, upset, or even threatening. He was just calm and patient. I told my dad about this person in the parking lot when I got back into the store, and he said that he was crazy. Now I'm wondering if he was one of the "Black Eyed People." I think he was.

Submitted by Ed R.

The incident took place about seven, or eight years ago. I have been reading many of the accounts on your website and wanted to share my story. It was a little different to the average account I have read and may be useful for someone. I had just moved to Las Vegas with my wife of twenty-years. We were small town folk from the Midwest. We moved cross-country. Being naive and new to city living, I habitually answered the door without a second thought. I had never even heard of a Black-Eyed Kid until this incident.

The first thing that should have tipped me off to the strangeness of this situation was the fact that someone was knocking at 4.30am. The second thing that should have dawned on me is this kid had to reach over a rather tall patio gate to unlatch and open it – which I tried to do later and couldn't manage. I'm not sure how he managed to get into my yard.

The knock at the door was startling. My wife and I were getting ready for work, a pretty normal routine. The moment I opened the door, I was overtaken with an inexplicable sense of fear. Literally I went from being relaxed to shaking like a leaf. To this day, I can picture him; a teenager, around five feet, average build, knee length black leather coat, short black hair and sunglasses. Eating an apple standing on the other side of my door.

He was very polite and asked if he could come in and warm up.

I said, No, closed the door and slid the security chain in to place.

A moment later, another knock.

I opened the now chained door, and before I could speak, he asked again if he could come in and warm up.

I said no again and attempted to close the door. Before the door could shut, he put his hand out stopping the door on its hinges.

He looked directly in to my eyes, still wearing his sunglasses, and said,

"Can I at least get some ketchup for my apple?"

"Not a chance," I replied. "My wife is currently calling the police."

He smiled and just said. "No! You won't be calling anybody."

At that moment, I pushed the door closed, locked it, and called out to my wife. She thought I had been talking to myself – she didn't even hear him talk. I pulled the curtains back to look out the window next to the door. He wasn't there. There was no trace of him. I go out on the patio and check the gate, but it's still latched from the inside.

My wife didn't believe me until that evening when she returned home and saw a half-eaten apple on the top step outside of our house. That's the freakiest bit. The damn half-eaten apple hadn't been there when I'd checked the yard – yet a few hours later it was sitting on my step waiting for us to return home.

Submitted by Anon.

I have been interested in the paranormal for a few years and read the stories on your site almost every day. I have been thinking about something that happened to me a couple of years ago. I was in college and had just left a movie theater with my boyfriend.

As we were leaving, I saw a car and I looked into the window, and no one was in it, or maybe the windows were tinted so I couldn't see anything, but I stared at it for a while not knowing why. Then my boyfriend realized he needed gas and he pulled over into a gas station. As he filled up and went into the station to pay for the gas, I noticed that the car I'd seen before had now pulled into the gas station and was pulled up against our car.

The window was rolling down and soon I could see a man, who looked to be a teenager, with long hair. I instantly thought he was just another kid getting gas. A coincidence. But when he turned to look at me, I could see that his eyes were completely black.

My first reaction was utter fear. I didn't feel like I was being looked at by just a kid. I just had a sensation. I turned away, too scared to look at him. Then I managed one more glance and he hadn't moved. He was still so close to his car window and had those eyes on me. I'll always remember those eyes.

When my boyfriend arrived, I told him about the guy. We both turned to look at the guy and he hadn't moved. He was in that same position. I noticed I wasn't the only one who couldn't keep looking at him. My boyfriend got freaked out too. We both had the same sensation: he's not human. I have since moved to another state, for work purposes, but I remember that incident very well.

Submitted by K Lyon

Here is another gas station encounter but please note that this one took place in the 1970's, long before such stories became popular.

I was heading home from a concert in the mid-1970's. I was about 120 miles away from home and I had to stop for gas. I pulled over and in front of the gas station, filled up and went inside to pay. I then decided that I had better go to the bathroom since I still had a bit of a drive ahead of me.

When I came back out, I went to grab a warm drink for the road. But when I turned around to pay, there was a man standing just a few feet behind me. He was wearing a business suit with a long black coat over that. When I went to pass him, he looked up at me. Where the eyes are supposed to be, there were only two big black holes. Everything else looked completely normal about this guy except he had no eyes. Just blackness.

I froze dead in my tracks. He continued to stare at me with a really intimidating stare. I finally caught my senses and just said, "Excuse me," walked on by up to the counter, handed him money, told him to keep the change and bolted out of there. The attendant didn't seem to be bothered by the man. I remember that he was more interested in the radio, than he was in what I, or the man, were doing.

The feeling that came over me upon seeing his face was nothing of this world. I had never felt it before — but I know it was 'pure' terror. An immediate sense of danger and dread like nothing I had ever experienced before. All I had in my mind was to get away as fast as possible.

Again, I never even mentioned anything about black-eyed people before I told my husband about this about twenty years later. He has been reading the accounts on your website, and one night told me about them. I freaked out and told him about what happened to me.

And yet another encounter that took place on the I-90.

This incident happened a little over two years ago, and I've never forgotten it. My husband and I were on our way up north on I-90 during the afternoon. Luckily, it was not at our normal time in the evening. We have a little place that we often go to for the weekends. As was our custom, we pulled in at our usual rest stop, and I went into the women's restroom. We had visited this place hundreds of times — so I had no concerns about using the restrooms.

As I was preparing to leave the room, I suddenly noticed a thin, dark-haired woman standing alone and staring directly at me. I instantly felt a terrible sense of dread, as though there was something deeply unnatural about her. I then noticed the eyes, which had been staring coldly at me, and they were completely black. I saw no color whatsoever and felt an extremely strong need to get away from her as quickly as possible, as there was something quietly threatening about her. Her stare was devoid of any emotion other than something very cold and disconnected.

*My instant and unwavering feeling during this
whole experience was that she was not in any way
human. I don't know what me made feel this so
strongly, but it was my most singular, strongest
sense while looking at her. There also was
something almost predatory about her, as though
she was homing in on prey while she stood there so
still. I also had a strange sense of her feeling
superior or stronger in some way. Again, the sense
of a predator watching its prey. I left as quickly as
possible, showing as little reaction to her as
possible. It seemed important, for some unknown
reason, for me to act unaffected by her while in her
presence. I felt a huge sense of relief as I got back
into the car and left. I have to say that this was one
of the most memorable brief experiences I've ever
had around a person, especially a stranger. I have
never been able to shake the unexplainable feeling
that she wasn't human.*

After many similar such experiences had been submitted, I felt
compelled to do some further research on the BEK and I discovered
that these kids and adults have been sighted persistently across the
USA for several years now. What I could not find in any numbers
however, were similar stories from other countries like, for example,
the UK. Yes, I could find stories of Black-Eyed humanoids, but the
whole story context is different, as we will see later. This type of
encounter or *modus operandi* seems to be more or less a US
phenomenon with just a small number of encounters in other
locations.

It is difficult to know when the BEK experiences first started being
reported but it seems commonly accepted on the Internet that the
phenomenon originated in one early account that appears on a ghost
related mailing list back in 1998. This account was written by Texas
reporter, Brian Bethel, relating supposed encounters with "black

eyed kids" in Abilene, Texas and Portland, Oregon. Bethel's stories gained massive popularity and in 2012, Bethel told his story on the reality television series *Monsters and Mysteries in America* and the rest is history, as they say. The original account can be read here, but his account is paraphrased by me below. His account follows much the same successfully terrifying format as all of the others in fact.

As he is sitting in his car, two children in their early teens approach him. He rolls down his car window and they ask him if they can get in, as they need a ride. He is immediately scared to death by these kids for no rational reason, but the calmness of the children and the incessant requests to be let in keep him from driving away or even winding up the window. He describes very well the feelings of foreboding and fear that he was experiencing and how compelled he felt to enter into this conversation. Every fiber in his body is telling him he is in danger and yet he cannot act on this. It is only when he sees that the kids have totally black eyes that he finds whatever strength it takes to break away and he races away in his car.

The story has all of the same compelling aspects of the ones submitted to us and he ends by asking a figurative question as to what may have happened to him had he let the kids into his car? The discussion of the encounter on the board contains some validation of his story in that one of the people involved in the discussion then relates a similar sinister story about a similar creepy encounter with these BEK. In fact, similar accounts to this supposed original one has also been submitted to the site. For example, how about this chilling experience?

> *I was on a date with my fiancé, who is now my husband, one night in 1985. This took place in New York City. Both my husband and I are lifelong New Yorkers. My husband is an accountant and I am a retired teacher. We were going to out to dinner and had just pulled over near to a restaurant we used to frequent quite a lot. As my husband parked the car outside the restaurant, we both heard someone knock their*

knuckles against the car window. Which is unusual as there is normally a doorman at this restaurant to dissuade that sort of thing. We both looked over and saw two teenage boys, in hoods standing outside our car. I immediately felt fear like I've never felt it before. My hands were shaking without any reason to shake. I was instantly petrified. The two boys were pale, from what I could see, and looked completely stoned. My immediate reaction was to leave, but my husband didn't want to leave without dinner. My husband opened the car door and the two boys stood back to let him out. He was just going to ignore them and go into the restaurant. I opened the door on my side of the car and got out too. When I turned around, I looked at the two boys and in the dim street light, they looked as though they just had black pools where their eyes should be. Just two large patches of black. No other color at all.

"We need a ride in your car," one of them said to my husband.

Mike, my husband, had actually turned his back to them to lock the car door. He hadn't seen their eyes.

"Well," he replied. "You're SOL."

"It won't take long," the boy said as though he didn't hear my husband's response. "We're just young people who need a ride."

That was so weird. Since when did teenagers call themselves young people? It was like two old men had jumped into these teenage bodies.

"Well... shit," my husband said at the time. He is a real New Yorker. "You better take the subway."

As my husband, Mike, turned the boys started screaming.

"Invite us into your car — we can't enter unless you invite us..."

My husband was about to yell back when he saw their eyes. His face completely fell. I have never seen him so shocked by something. He side stepped away from them and moved onto the sidewalk. I moved to the back of our car. We both watched as these two boys suddenly started screaming and shouting. The two boys backed up still screaming and shouting.

"You need to let us in," one of them screamed pointing at us. "We have to see our friend."

We turned around and headed into the restaurant. The doorman was standing inside the lobby. He hadn't seen or heard the boys. We had dinner, and I thought that would be the end of it.

I remember feeling terrified for days after. I didn't sleep very well and had a lot of nightmares. I had a lot of headaches too. A week later and I was starting to dread going to bed as I would see these boys every single time, I opened my eyes I was worried they would visit us again or appear in our bedroom. I was scared to leave the house, and I felt *violated – as though they had attacked me. Yet, all they had done was nothing compared to what others have gone through. They really didn't do much except scream, shout and act weird. It was what happened to me afterwards that really bothered me. I really think that once you get caught up with these kids, they have a long-lasting effect on you. Nightmares, panic attacks, sleepwalking, headaches, fear of seeing them again.*

A few months later and things were starting to calm down. I asked my husband if he remembered the incident. He said he did, and he had met up with them again. Apparently, they were outside his office one afternoon waiting by his car. They did the same thing they did outside the restaurant. When my husband told them, he was calling the police from his office the kids didn't seem to care one way, or another. The creepiest thing was that they told him they wanted to go to an address to visit their friend who could help them. The address at the time didn't mean anything – it was just a suburb of New Jersey. Years later we were moving to a new house and when my husband saw the address of the house, I wanted him to see he went white. It was the same address those boys had told him about outside of his office.

What are these kids? What do they want? Some say they're demons, others say they are lost spirits? I have no idea what they are – but they terrified the hell out of me.

However, as we have already seen, Bethel's account wasn't actually the earliest report of encounters with black-eyed people. In fact, as we will see later, black-eyed humanoids appear throughout much of human history.

The Internet is full of similar stories to Bethels'. It appears that hundreds, if not thousands, of people across the USA have had an encounter with these mysterious and menacing BEK. There is even an entire Reddit group devoted to such stories and many, often incredible theories abound about what they are and what they might want.

In one widely reported instance, the BEK were allowed in to the home and with disastrous consequences. The story of the encounter follows the now all too familiar horrifying sequence of an unexpected knock at the door at 2am. Two small children stand there and the man answering the door inexplicably was totally unnerved by them. Thinking the kids had got lost or perhaps there had been an accident, he lets the kids in and his wife makes cocoa for them. He keeps asking them what has happened, and they keep on repeating, *"not to worry as their parents would be there soon."*

The scared and concerned couple started to notice that their pets were behaving strangely. The husband began also to feel dizzy and strange as he sat with the kids. When the woman of the house returns with the cocoa, she almost drops it when they look at her and she sees that their eyes are completely black. At this point the kids ask to use the bathroom and husband and wife start to discuss the scene. His nose starts bleeding profusely. Then, just as inexplicably, the power goes out and they find themselves in darkness. They stand in the darkness in total fear until suddenly, the kids leave abruptly saying that their parents had arrived leaving the front door wide open. Outside, the woman can see a car idling on the street and two tall, dark suited adults. After a while, the power came back on.

After that, nothing was the same. The cats disappeared. The pet bird died of a hemorrhage in a pool of blood in its cage. The husband's nosebleeds became progressively worse and he was then diagnosed with skin cancer meanwhile the wife also began to suffer dizzy spells and nosebleeds. Had the encounter with the BEK caused this?

This strange and sinister testimony resulted in suggestions in some quarters that the BEK were some form of soul eaters or demons.

Their hypnotic effect keeping a terrified victim who somehow senses the danger, transfixed. The BEK want to get close to their intended victim and more importantly, they want you to grant permission to let them in. Let them in to what? Your soul?

The BEK suck your life energy; feed off of it. Given permission to come in, they devour your soul. Let's face facts. In this modern era, many people don't know or believe that they have a soul and they do little to protect or preserve it. They would never believe that other creatures may want it from you and by the time they realize this, it is too late.

Other than one other story that you can find on the Internet that I have paraphrased above, this is the only experience that I can find after many hours of searching in which the BEK successfully gain entry to a home. In the other story, the person relating the experience has the familiar BEK experience one evening and tells them to go away. His neighbors are not seen for days and eventually are found to have vanished without a trace. The person telling the story raises the possibility that the same BEK had gone to his neighbors and they had let them in. All conjecture of course and no evidence whatsoever is presented to suggest that the story can be taken as truth.

However, one has only to consider how few stories there are in which these BEK were allowed entry to start to think that perhaps those who did let them in potentially suffered some horrifying fate. Some 90,000 people have simply disappeared at any given time in the USA, never to be heard from again. One also wonders if at least some of these people fell victim to the BEK?

In some instances, it would seem as if the energy sucking nature of the BEK begins just by having contact with them even though entry is not permitted. Here is an example.

One morning during breakfast there was a knock on the door. I opened it to find two boys, around 10-12, standing on my porch. The taller boy had knocked, the smaller had been straddling a bike. I found this odd that he was on my porch on his bike. He would have had to carry it up my front steps, and instead of standing beside it, was sitting on it. Still, kids are kids, right?

At first, they kept their heads down, and I asked if I could help them. They said they just needed to come in for a minute and it wouldn't take long. I asked if they were from the neighborhood, and they didn't answer. It was about this time that I realized something wasn't right.

I told them that I wasn't comfortable letting them into our house. There had been a number of home invasions and both my wife and I, were wary of strangers. They didn't say anything else. However, the strange stuff started happening after they left.

I kept having recurring nightmares about their visit, which would wake me in the middle of the night. I completely lost my appetite and I didn't want to leave my house. Then they visited me again. It was morning during breakfast and my wife heard someone knock on the door. She went to answer it and saw the boys I had mentioned standing there waiting for her.

They stood and stared at her, and she stared back.

"He will die," one of them said. "Soon."

My wife told them to get the hell off our property and they just smiled at her.

"Let us in to use the phone," he said.

My wife said that she had never been so scared in her life. She just stepped back, closed the door and turned around. She came back into the kitchen and asked me if I had heard them. I told her I hadn't. I had thought she was in the bedroom.

I kept feeling awful and about a week after that incident I went to see my doctor. He then sent me to a doctor for tests. They found that I had a tumor. They operated, and I survived – but I believe that it was caused by those damn kids. I think that they are demonic. They are also telepathic as during my encounter I had thought, "what's happening here?" The taller boy looked at me with those black eyes and said directly into my head...

"You know he isn't real don't you'?"

Stay away from these damn kids – seriously.

Probably extremely good advice!

The Black-Eyed Kid Phenomenon Elsewhere
When I told you at the beginning of the book that the first story
submitted to the My Haunted Life Too website was the one that
captured everyone's morbid fascination I wasn't lying. I wasn't
telling the full truth however. The fact is that we had a Black-Eyed
Kid encounter story submitted several months prior. It went like this,

*My brother was in his room talking to someone,
which I thought was strange as we were alone in
our house. I went to see whom he was talking to.
There was no one there when I looked, so I asked
him whom he was talking to, and he said the little
girl with the black eyes. That freaked me out a
little.*

*Nothing happened for a while after that, about a
week went by then we started hearing voices and
footsteps. I would be sleeping with my blankets all
wrapped up around me, and I would wake up with
them folded neatly at the bottom of my bed.*

*My sister got scared one night and crawled into
bed with me. As she was getting into my bed, I
woke up and couldn't fall back asleep, so I turned
on my TV. I also turned on my light to find the
remote. I left the light on along with the TV. Right
when we were both drifting off to sleep, my door
slammed shut, which is almost impossible, as I
always have a basket full of books in front of the
door so that it doesn't close, my light shut off, and
my TV went all fuzzy and made that static noise.*

*I ran and tried to open my door, which can only
lock from the inside, it is a push lock, so all you
have to do is turn the handle, and it unlocks.
Anyway, I tried to open my door, but it was like*

someone was holding the door handle from the outside.

My sister and I screamed as loud as we could, then my mom came and opened the door. Just then the light flipped back on, the TV was on and the basket was set back up. We've tried blessing the house and praying, as we are very Christian.

The 'house' we live in was built in 2003, and no one has died there. We don't know what to do.

Submitted by Eden

At the time, this seemed like a more 'normal' haunting experience in which the ghost had black eyes. You will note that none of the typical BEK encounter story aspects or *modus operandi* are included. It is just a haunting. Except that once I started to research the BEK, I discovered that BEK stories from other countries are more usually of this nature. They do not follow the tried and tested familiar pulse-racing formula of those reported across the US. In fact, there has been a similar furor about BEK's in the UK fueled by lurid stories in the media. However, these BEK are ghosts, phantasms, apparitions and quite clearly not innocent looking physical kids standing on your doorstep.

One widely reported example from the UK involves the Black-Eyed Child of Cannock Chase in the Midlands of England.

As reported in the Birmingham Mail[1],

Alerted by what sounded like screams, a shocked woman came across the wandering, sightless

---

[1]   http://www.birminghammail.co.uk/news/midlands-news/black-eyed-child-returns-haunt-7846214

spectre while walking Birches Valley.

*"We instantly started running towards the noise,"
she said. "We couldn't find the child anywhere and
so stopped to catch our breath.*

*"That's when I turned around and saw a girl stood
behind me, no more than 10 years old, with her
hands over her eyes.*

"It was as if she was waiting for a birthday cake".

*"I asked if she was OK and if she had been the one
screaming. She put her arms down by her side and
opened her eyes.*

*"That's when I saw they were completely black, no
iris, no white, nothing.*

*"I jumped back and grabbed my daughter. When I
looked again, the child was gone. It was so
strange."*

The article goes on to describe a similar encounter back in 1982 in
the same location with a Black-Eyed girl in which there was even a
manhunt for the child organized by the local police. The story was
picked up by several other national UK media outlets and pretty
soon, people were reporting BEK ghosts all around the UK. There
was, as the media kept on reporting, a plague of BEK ghosts in the
UK.

Author and researcher, David Weatherly, has also reported on a very
early encounter in his book on *Black Eyed Kids*[2] in France. In this

---

[2] David Weatherley, The Black Eyed Children, Leprechaun Press, 2012

story from 1974, two men driving their car came across five small figures by a house in the country standing huddle together in a group. The men stopped the car and wound down the window to get a closer look at these strange creatures. Their blood ran cold at what they saw. The creatures were humanoid, small with long dark dank hair. Their eyes set in a yellowish skin, were as black as coal. One of the creatures indicated to them to come closer but the two men were beset with an overwhelming fear and sped off in total fright.

A long search of the Internet did result in a few stories of a similar nature in places like Australia, France and other western nations, but it is the US that the vast majority of traditional BEK stories come from. Outside of the US, the stories are often more about ghosts and ghouls that have no eyes or black eyes, just like those that created such a furor in the UK.

One BEK story we received though was from the UK. However, a visiting American submitted it and it follows the usual format as follows,

> *I have been following the stories you have been posting about these Black-Eyed Kids. Just a few months ago, I was travelling in Europe. I'm from Michigan but had the once in a lifetime opportunity to go to Europe with a friend. I was enjoying my vacation – until this happened.*

> *One weekend I heard crying from the hallway of my hotel room. I lay on my back in bed a little while, thinking about what it could be. My friend was sleeping like the dead, so I got out of bed to go check out the crying. I was about to be scared half to death.*

> *I got out of our room and went toward the main door and opened it up. I stuck my head out and looked both left and right. I wish I hadn't. Down*

the hallway stood a little girl, wearing a white nightdress, with her hair in front of her face.

I got out on the hallway and got closer to the girl. Slowly, she turned and raised her face. She wiped her hair from out of her eyes. Two pitch-black spots where her eyes should've been, stared at me. She started smiling. I could see that her teeth were almost similar to a vampire.

After a little while, she stopped giggling and there was quiet in the hall for a minute. I turned back to my room and closed the door behind me. I couldn't hear anything outside until the knocking started. It started gently with just a few taps and got progressively louder.

"Let me in," a voice called out.

I said nothing.

"Let me in!"

My friend was still fast asleep. The "little girl" was screaming and shouting, knocking on the door.

"Let me in," she kept screaming. "I need to come inside."

It was like there was a storm in the hallway. I closed my eyes and started crying. The knocking and screaming lasted for an hour or so, and then died away. The next morning, I asked my friend why she hadn't woken up – she had no idea what I was talking about. I know from the stories I've been reading on here that I encountered a Black-Eyed Kid. I also know that these incidents are real – and terrifying.

Submitted by J R

Although there are similarities in the encounter format, the girl seems to have black holes for eyes as opposed to black eyes. Was this a physical child or a Black-Eyed ghost? Are they different phenomenon?

The Meaning of Black Eyes

I have found other stories that involve people developing black eyes when angry or as part of a fit of rage. The idea is, I suppose, that black eyes are demonic and that this anger is evil such that the person takes on some demonic qualities like those menacing and soulless black eyes. Here, for example, is an account given in an article called *The Eyes of a Sociopath* by Donna Anderson[3].

One occurrence to this day puts chills up my spine and tears in my eyes.

The night my husband held me at gunpoint with a loaded hunting rifle, something terrifying happened. My husband's eyes are bright, light blue. He has beautiful eyes, so bright you notice them from across a room.

But that night, when he attacked me, his eyes were black. Not just black but so black it goes beyond words. If you've ever watched the movie AMITYVILLE HORROR, there's a scene when the father has become deeply possessed and he turns on his family.

MY SPOUSE LOOKED 100% IDENTICAL TO THAT MAN!

AFTER THE INCIDENT, I BEGAN TO QUESTION MY SANITY. BLUE EYES DON'T TURN BLACK. EYES CHANGE COLOR, BUT NO HUMAN HAS EYES LIKE THAT.

---

[3] http://www.lovefraud.com/2014/10/27/the-eyes-of-a-sociopath/

I researched it, and lo and behold there have been numerous cases dealing with narcissists and/or sociopaths where blue eyes were noted to have turned black when they were enraged!

How horrifying is that? It's as though there is another being inside these people!

I still have nightmares. Never before nor since has he ever demonstrated that behaviour. He says he doesn't remember any of it. (No, I don't think drugs and I know no alcohol was involved.)

In fact, there are many accounts of people's eyes turning black when angry on the Internet however, what is happening most usually is that the person's pupils dilate to such a degree as to look as if they have developed an all-black eye. In most instances, that is all that is occurring, but there is also an insinuation that, in that moment of anger and hysterics, they are taken over by a demonic entity.

A common Hollywood movie technique to indicate possession, or alien affinity, is to have the character have black eyes either permanently or periodically. After the possession is over or the spell is broken, the eyes return to normal. Somehow, black eyes are considered to be a sign of evil or malevolence and this theme is echoed in the BEK phenomenon. The eyes are the gateway to the soul and when those eyes are black or, just like reflective sunglasses, dark and opaque, it elicits a certain response of fear, distaste and foreboding. Just like this experience submitted to the My Haunted Life Too website.

I was riding the bus back home after work. It was about 6am. I'm a security guard and often work odd hours. So, I'm sitting there, and this guy gets on and sits across from me. He was wearing a suit and had a briefcase but was a regular looking guy in his 30s. What struck me about him at first was that he was chewing a cigar, not smoking it; you can't smoke on the bus. So, I was just looking at him while he stared out the window and chewed his cigar, and all of a sudden, he turned and looked at me. His eyes were absolutely pitch black, just as others have described.

My heart started beating, and I felt the hair on the back of my neck standing straight up. I was starting to panic, and I had no idea why, I was terrified of this guy. Then he grinned at me, and his teeth were all covered in tobacco bits and brown juice, the cigar clamped between them. I almost screamed, but instead I had the presence of mind to just get up and take the seat right behind the driver. I calmed down a bit after that, but I kept an eye on the guy. He ended up chatting with some girl that got on, and they were still talking when I got off.

This Black-Eyed Person experience lacks the characteristics of the typical encounter but the very idea that someone's eyes would be totally black still elicits the same fear response. Here is another example encounter with a Black-Eyed Person.

The bar was packed six people deep, loud music, and what looked like no end to the drink callouts. My husband, Jim, looked up and saw a tall man slowly approaching the bar. He was approx. 6 ft. 5 in. tall with long, straight black hair. He wore black trousers, t-shirt, and long black coat. Jim said it was as if the crowd parted for this man as he slowly walked straight up to the bar, smack bang in front of Jim's frozen gaze.

He quietly ordered bourbon. When Jim looked up at this huge man, he noticed his eyes were completely black. Jim turned to make the drink and glanced in the mirror, looking at the black-eyed man just staring back.

Jim mustered enough courage to turn and give him the drink.

Jim said he felt great fear at first while in his presence. He knew this man was staring at him, but he didn't want to make eye contact, but felt compelled not to feel fear.

The large black-eyed man knocked back the bourbon and disappeared into the crowd. Jim, for unknown reason, had a feeling to run after him for what he believes was to ask the large man what he wanted, what he was doing there, or who he was he after. Jim moved as quickly as he could through crowd of people on two levels of the club to get to the front door.

The strange man was nowhere in sight. Jim asked the security staff, but no one saw him leave. No bar staff saw the huge black-eyed man. No one. Jim was baffled how the barman next to him did not see him, nor did any of the regulars at the bar. Security tapes also showed nothing.

What the hell did Jim see?

In this experience, the black eyes are combined with a mysterious disappearing act and the effect is both deeply sinister and strange. Other variations on the story have been submitted also – this one from Australia.

I have been reading a lot of stories about the Black-Eyed People lately. I want to share my experience with one of them. This took place in March 2007. I live in Australia and March is the beginning of fall, but the nights can still be quite warm. I was working at a coffee shop in the city at the time and decided to walk home that night. It would take me around forty-five minutes to walk home but figured, what the hey.

I was about half way home and it was already dark. It would have been about 7 p.m. I was just walking past my local library when I noticed a homeless guy who I'd seen around our neighborhood the last few months. He was heading toward me up the sidewalk.

I knew I didn't like this guy because he was always grinning and staring at me and as I came closer, I made a point of avoiding eye contact. For some reason, as I was passing him, I looked up and into his eyes. They were completely black. Just as the other encounters have mentioned– there was not a single speck of white to be found in his eyes.

He was also grinning at me, all teeth bared, and I instantly felt like turning to run. I mean these people absolutely make you feel terrified. It's like nothing I can explain. Even your bones feel shaky.

I remember being shocked and scared and I raced home as fast as I could. I turned back once, and he was just standing there staring after me. When I got home, I told my boyfriend, but he brushed me off. I don't know who or what this guy was, but I've never forgotten it, and neither will you if you run into them.

Submitted by K Walters

Again, the black eyes cause fear and confusion in the beholder. Black eyes are not normal, and, in popular mythology and legend, they indicate malevolence and demonic possession. Just to reinforce the point, here is an experience submitted to the site that isn't about black-eyed kids at all but nonetheless, it features blacked out eyes.

In the 90's in London, England, my daughter rented a house from a landlord. It was a two bedroom as she has three children. Everything seemed fine at first, but her two youngest boys kept telling her that there was something nasty in the house. She didn't believe them, and thought they were making it up.

The house happened to be near a cemetery. One evening, after she had taken the children to bed, she told me that she came out of the bedroom and a great big black figure was standing just outside the door.

It had no visible face. She said that it must have been an entity. She was terrified, and it just gradually disappeared.

Another time, she took a photo on her camera phone when she visited me. She said, "Look at that, mum!" In the picture, the youngest child was on the sofa, but down near his feet was a small, hooded figure, and my grandson's eyes had been blacked out with black tape.

My husband and I suggested that my daughter leave. She eventually agreed.

Finally, here is an account of an encounter that has some of the usual storyline included – but not all.

I am a fifty-year-old man who lives in Cincinnati, Ohio. I work as a real estate broker and spend a lot of time around people. I have never seen anything like the kids I met to show around an apartment six months ago.

An apartment came free to rent in a good part of town. I had shown it to several people – but had one more appointment to show it that day. I was waiting just inside the doors of the complex when I saw two kids walk up to the apartment building. Even though it was a sunny day, I knew as soon as I saw them that I was not going to let them in. One of them was young boy of about 17 or 18, approximately. He knocked on the glass and stared at me. I stood absolutely still and said nothing. He asked me about an open apartment for rent. I remember feeling very scared and shaken by his appearance. He did not look weird by his dress or such. It was his eyes. I remember feeling the hair on my neck stand up, and I was shaking just from looking in his eyes.

I have never felt like this before in all the years I have done this job. I could not look him straight in the eyes. I felt like I was about to die. My instincts told me this. I noticed a third kid was walking up behind them with a bicycle. The two boys standing on the other side of the door did not move toward me or anything, but he was just waiting for me to invite him in or take him to the empty unit.

Now, some people may think that I was just over-reacting or something, but the eyes were completely black, like there was no real pupil. He spoke normally to me, but I had to just step into the apartment building office to my right. I had to get out of his face and get as far from him as I could. I felt like I was in extreme danger. Only because of the eyes. I think if I had looked any longer into them, I would have not been able break his gaze.

I shook for several hours after that. I called my daughter at work and told her about it. She told me about the black-eyed kids. I am still afraid of that image of his eyes.

Here we have the black eyes, the debilitating fear and also the let them enter aspects of the usual encounter. Do the BEK live among us in apartments and homes they have rented, or was this just a different *modus operandi* to gain entry and access to a victim?

Black Eyes in Mythology and Soul Eaters

Black eyes are not just used to denote evilness or possession in movies and urban legends, but also feature widely in occult mythology. For example, the Iroquois Indians believed in a dark power called the Otkon that could take over children and an 'Evil One' who would mate with human females to produced black-eyed, chalky skinned, children. These children were killed by the tribe soon after birth and burned to stop them from resurrecting. Children wandering alone in the woods could also be taken over by Otkon and would re-emerge with black eyes and pale skin acting nervously while repeating themselves over and over. Their goal was to destroy the tribe and infect all of the people with Otkon. Could this be the true origin of the BEK urban legend in America?

A common feature of the BEK is that they ask permission to enter. It has been long held as a truism that certain demons and vampires do indeed need permission to cross your threshold. This concept has been a part of shows like *Buffy The Vampire Slayer,* for example, and is a part of our urban mythology. The constant demands to be allowed in to a person's home, car or whatever on the part of the BEK is a deliberate request for permission to enter and, as we have seen, once allowed in, horrible things seem to happen to the person that gave them permission. Does this mean that without your permission, the BEK cannot harm you? Perhaps, however, there are numerous stories in which an encounter with the BEK has left the person tried, drained and feeling as if they have been sucked of energy.

Here is the perfect example of the need for permission to enter recently submitted.

> *This story is about a black-eyed salesman that my family and I encountered a few years ago. It was an ordinary day. My mom, father, one of my brothers and I were in the living room watching TV.*

All of a sudden, we heard a knock on the door, which is strange because we had a fully functioning doorbell. I walked to the door and looked in the peephole and saw a black man, probably in his forties, with a black suit on and a long black trench coat over that.

He creeped me out because I kept asking who it was, but he never responded. I could just see him trying to look into the peephole from outside. So, I told my father to come to the door. My father opened the door and I immediately felt fear for some reason. The man was not saying or doing anything in particular to make me feel this way, but it's just the feeling I got.

My father asked what he wanted, and he said he had some kitchenware for sale and would like to know if we wanted to purchase some.

My father signaling for the guy to come in, but he just kept peeking around the corner as if he was checking it out before he entered. My father looked at him and said, "Aren't you going to show us what you've got?"

The guy kept saying, still looking around, "Only if you invite me in."

"I opened the door," my father said.

"I know, but you have to invite me in," the man replied.

Looking baffled, my father said, "Come in."

As the guy entered, he kept staring at me, and I noticed that he had no whites in his eyes. They were totally black! No life in them at all. My father never bought anything from him and he never took anything out of his bag. He just kept telling my father that if he bought from him, he would be eternally grateful for his purchase. My father asked him to leave because he never showed him what he would be purchasing.

The creepy part is that when I opened my eyes as he was leaving, he was still staring at me, and my mom said he stared at me the entire time he talked. No one knew I was praying, but I felt that this guy could sense it. It was as if he was bothered by it.

After he left, we started smelling the scent of fresh roses and flowers. The guy had never even taken anything out of his bag, so that was strange. We immediately looked out the window to see if he was there, he should have just been leaving our porch at this time. But no one was there. I went outside to see if maybe he went to a neighbor's house, but he was nowhere to be found.

He came back about a month or two later when I was home alone. He had on the same outfit, all black eyes, and same bag. This time I never opened the door or let him in. I peeked through the peephole only to find him peeking back, smiling sinisterly.

And once again he just disappeared. I'm happy to say that I have never seen him again.

Then there was this rather strange encounter.

I had just been shaken to the core by a UFO encounter. I was left shocked, nervous, and a bit afraid, but also in awe by this encounter. I decided to report this to Mufon. A mufon investigator came to my home and I told him about my sighting which he seemed to find very interesting and amazing.

Two days later there was a knock at my door. There stood a very young man holding some magazines. The magazines looked a little tattered and somewhat used. He was looking down as he talked to me saying he was a magazine salesman. His tone of voice was drone-like. I was very nervous the minute I opened the door and somewhat afraid. Why, I don't really know.

As the young man looked up at me, I noticed he had large square black glasses on and his eyes were large and pitch black. His face was pale white and waxy looking. So, eerie and not at all human looking. He stared at me with intensity. That scared me even more. Not to mention the magazines he was selling were old and torn. The black suit he had on was very much out of style and looked to be from the 1950's. The young man proceeded to say he needed to come in, so he could show me the magazines. I told him he could show me from the front porch. He persisted that he needed to come inside. He repeated that several times and began to become irritated with me. I told him I wasn't interested but he continued to want to come in. He wouldn't give up. I was scared and wanted him to leave but he wouldn't. He said I needed to invite him in or else he wasn't allowed to enter, which I thought was a strange thing to say.

Not allowed??? He began to step inside. He said again I needed to invite him in with such urgency in his voice that it frightened me. I had to push him away and slam the door and lock it. The man kept knocking on the door saying he had to come in. I yelled to him to go away or I would call the police. All of a sudden it was very quiet. The knocking had stopped. I walked to the window and looked out. There was NOBODY THERE! It seemed impossible that he could of disappear that quick.

I was left feeling very scared and shocked at what had just happened. It was the strangest thing!

The next day I asked my neighbors if they had a magazine salesman come to their door. The answer I got from all of them was, " no". They said they hadn't even seen anyone around the neighborhood that fit that description.

I don't think he was a real salesman at all. He looked, sounded and acted very very strange. Those huge black eyes were one of the scariest things I'd ever seen. He just seemed so odd and robot like. I hope I never see anyone like that again. Unreal.

As for being paranormal, I couldn't say. Maybe it had something to do with the ufo I had seen two days earlier. All I know is it was extremely strange and very scary!!!

Submitted by Paula

This story has a UFO connection and plainly the person relating the experience is questioning an alien affinity for the BEK. However, Myth and legend is also replete with soul eaters or beings that live off the souls of men. These dark shadowy beings are sometimes described as having black eyes or have no eyes at all – just dark holes were their eyes should be.

Consider this also, in Native American folklore, an *Acheri* is the ghost or spirit of a little girl who comes down from mountains and hilltops at night to bring sickness to humans, particularly children. They are often depicted with dark or unnatural eyes and can also be referred to as "hill fairies". The *Acheri* is said to bring death to the elderly or other people with low immune system defenses. The boogieman in many cultures will have black eyes.

Are the BEK then a form of soul eating Demon? Are they simply a modern manifestation of a whole host of semi-mythical occult creatures that seek permission to enter (you) and have certain strange physical characteristics that mark them out as not entirely human - like black eyes?

What are the BEK?

Researching the BEK, one finds many theories as to what they could be. Some think it all to be an urban legend, like the Slender man, created back in 1998 by Brian Bethel (although, I have said that Brian Bethel's account is not the first), others suspect it may just be a prank by kids wearing black eye lenses - possibly in order to sustain the myth. There are also some wild theories that they are the product of interbreeding between aliens and humans where they have inherited the eyes of the alien race that abducted humans for experimentation and DNA manipulation. However, the better theories, in my view, are that they are some kind of manifestation of demonic activity, as discussed above.

Despite the assertions by many on the Internet that all stories of the BEK come after the original Brain Bethel encounter, there is enough evidence to show that this is incorrect. 1998 just happens to coincide with growing access to the Internet that helped to propagate stories, accounting for the sudden surge in numbers of people reporting these terrifying encounters. Prior to that, such experiences would be difficult to discuss or document in a public forum, but there are stories of Black-Eyed people and ghosts encountered before 1998 and we have produced a couple of examples previously. In fact, in my humble opinion, the BEK seem to be the latest manifestation of demonic beings that seek to take away your soul. Similar beings have been documented throughout history, albeit with slightly different characteristics, depending upon the culture and time that they were experienced. There was always a bogeyman somewhere in the darkness or in the woods waiting to steal the soul, and perhaps life, of the unsuspecting innocent. The BEK seem to me to be just the modern, mass media via the Internet, version of that mythological creature.

On the other hand, the BEK stories share many similarities and attributes and there is no doubt that it could all be just an urban myth originating in the Hollywood horror-fed USA. The black eyes, the hypnotic effect, the heart pounding feeling of terror, the permission to enter all combine to make for a good chilling story that can keep you awake at night fearing the worst. Just one problem with this idea in my view – there are simply so many people who genuinely claim to have encountered these beings. Even if 90% were made up or fanciful, then what are the remainder? Another theory is that they are inter-dimensional beings, but no evidence is provided to substantiate this.

In my web-based research, I came across one report that purported to come from an actual BEK. The person making this claim suggested that the BEK were direct descendants of Lilith, the original demon. They had existed throughout time living alongside its human prey that had been created more or less as automaton humans and would exist long after humanity had gone. The authenticity of this account is however, questionable at best.

In what seemed like a final twist to this eerie story, we recently received another puzzling encounter with a final and spine chilling, but intriguing twist.

This account of the Black-Eyed Kids is a little unusual. My experience took place several months ago, in Kansas. I have been reading the other accounts on your site and wanted to share my story here.

Looking back, the most bizarre thing about my experience was how quickly they showed up. I walked in the porch, turned around to lock it, then turned back, and there was a knock. More than anything else about this story, that freaks me out. It's not something I've seen in other accounts that I've read.

I turned around and saw them: two kids, one was in his early teens. The other looked about eleven. The older one was knocking. He looked panicked and was really pounding on the door. The younger one looked emotionless and didn't say anything.

"We have to use your phone!"

I felt my hand moving forward, towards the doorknob, but then I yanked it back. I don't know if I need to explain that I "wanted to help them, but also felt afraid of them," but I did. It's in all the encounters, so I'm just confirming that, yes, it happened to me too. These kids absolutely strike fear into your heart.

It's always seemed strange to me that no one who's ever encountered the Black-Eyed Kids has ever heard of them before. I had at least read a few paranormal websites, and I knew of a few of the stories people had told. I think that's why it was like reflex when I heard a request to use the phone; my eyes went to theirs, and I saw that they were solid black. And I knew what these kids were.

The older kid seemed to immediately realize what I'd seen. I've heard that they usually get mad if you see their eyes. That didn't happen this time, though. His eyes got a look of desperation.

"I swear to God I won't hurt you!" he screamed. "You can trust us."

That's something I've never seen reported before.

I ran to get my shotgun. I wasn't going to just stand there and listen to them begging to get in for the next hour.

When I came back with the gun, though, they were already gone. In their place was a young girl. Her hair was very light. I remember it as white. She wasn't trying to get in. In fact, she was looking away. I pointed the gun at her anyway.

"You get the hell out of here!"

"You don't need to do that," she said, "I don't even want to get in."

I lowered my gun involuntarily. This girl freaked me out far more than the boys did, but I was powerless to disobey her. She had power.

"There were some boys who came by and asked to come into your house. Is that correct?"

"Yes," I said. I hoped that being honest with her would get her to go away as soon as possible.

"How long ago did they leave?"

"Just now. I was going to get my gun for them, and when I came back you were here."

"Excellent, then they should still be close. Don't worry, you won't be seeing them again."

She turned to me briefly, and I caught a glimpse of her face. I looked at the eyes, expecting them to be black again. Instead, I saw they were pure white. No irises, and no pupils. Just pure, white pools in her face, that seemed to glow slightly in the darkness.

She turned and walked away, and I realized something; I believed her. I fully expected that I would've never seen those boys again.

Submitted by BI

And then there was this encounter recently submitted too.

I live in Indianapolis, Indiana, in the United States, and this is where this event took place in February of 1988. My girlfriend, myself, and a couple of friends were out bar hopping on a Friday night, just having a good time. I ran out of cash and had to run to the ATM at the bank down the block. I made it to the ATM and withdrew some cash, and this was when things got weird.

I turned around and saw that across the street was a man leaning against the telephone pole on the corner. He was dressed well, in a black suit with an open-collar maroon shirt. He was tall, white with short, jet-black hair. I'm couldn't be sure at that distance, but I firmly believe that his eyes were completely jet-black. The scariest part was that he was staring across this crowded intersection at me with this incredibly smug look on his face.

I didn't want to hang around any longer than I had to, so I took off at a quick pace back toward the club where my friends were. After several yards, I allowed myself a glance backward and saw that he was following me across the street. I reminded myself that nothing could happen with people all around, but I didn't really believe it. I reached the club, but there was a line in front of the bouncer who was checking IDs. I stood there shaking with fear as I saw the man pause on the other side of the street, look both ways, then calmly begin crossing toward me. Every move he made was precise and deliberate. I knew that when he got to me something horrible was going to happen, and it was only with great effort that I managed to maintain my composure.

Just then, another man walked up to me from the other direction. He was in his late 20s or early 30s, wearing jeans, sneakers, a baseball cap, and a hooded sweatshirt from a local university. He touched me on the shoulder and I immediately felt calmer. Then, he said, "Don't worry. You're all right. We have everything under control." I glanced back at the man in the suit and he had paused in the middle of the street. It's amazing that he wasn't run over. The sweatshirt man turned away from me to face the man in the suit. It was clear to me that this was a showdown. After a moment, the man in the suit sneered at us, in frustration, it seemed. Then turned around and walked away. The sweatshirt man turned back to me with a reassuring smile, patted my shoulder and walked on.

Are the Black-Eyed Kids hunted by another group of sinister beings with white eyes? Who are the WEK? and what are they? How do they relate to the BEK?

There are now a number of stories on the Internet about white-eyed kids and people. Is this simply a new twist in an old and tested formula? Or, are these WEP somehow related to the BEK? One answer postulated by some observers is that the eye color is an indication of demonic rank. Black eyes are said to indicate the worker or common demons, while white eyes signify a sort of superior demon or boss demon if you will. If so, why is it that one group seems to hunt the other? Certainly, the WEK seem much more powerful than the BEK, though sharing all the same features except for the white eyes.

Some of the reports of White Eyed Kids that I have read in my research seem to suggest that the WEK are more adept at mind control and exhibit other phenomena like levitation for example. In some of the experiences with WEK, the kids had super human strength despite being small and innocent looking. The children mostly have White hair or Blond hair and are usually around 9 to 16 years of age. Most of the reports apparently originate in rural areas and noticeably from around Native American areas. No one knows much about the WEK though at the moment and we will need to watch and see how the story unfolds.

So, what are the BEK? Well, your guess is as good as mine, but I do think it is fair to make the following observations;

1. BEK stories certainly predate the Internet and certainly there are stories of encounters that predate the 1989 date of Brain Bethel's now famous posting, despite what you may read elsewhere.
2. In fact, even the term BEK is misleading. There are as many stories of black-eyed adults as there are of black-eyed kids. There seems to be a race of beings that have, or can develop, black eyes.
3. By and large, most stories of the BEK originate in the USA though not all. There are a disproportionate number of accounts of encounters in America. Other black-eyed being sightings, like those of Cannock Chase, for example, seem to be different and lack the definite characteristics of the common BEK encounter. The common characteristic between all of the encounters is black eyes or no eyes and that is where the similarities mostly end.
4. There are few stories of exactly what happens to people who let the BEK into their homes. Why is that? Are the BEK actually incompetent? Or is the answer more sinister still?

Could some of the 90,000 missing Americans at any point in time have been victims of the BEK?

5. The encounters with black-eyed people follow a similar format. Entry is required. There is an element of hypnosis involved and there is that fear! Yet, this formula is actually one that has been used for many hundreds of years by many cultures to define their bogeymen. There is an element of formula and myth in these BEK encounter stories.

6. Occult mythology is full of beings that steal your soul, steal your life force and these beings are often endowed with black eyes. Are the BEK a more recent incarnation of these creatures?

7. Although there are many theories about who and what the BEK may be, the best fitting one is that of a demonic entity in my opinion – soul eaters – who need permission to cross the threshold and feed on your energy, life force or soul. Despite this, there is also an aspect of the urban legend here too. Undoubtedly, some if not many of these stories are made up, fanciful or mistaken. But are they all? I sincerely doubt it.

8. The BEK appear to have power to disrupt electricity supply, phones and more. The WEK can have a much more impactful effect on their surroundings. These are all powers associated with demonic forces.

9. The BEK are often only seen or heard by their intended victim yet they seem to be physical beings. In some accounts, they have walked through walls or simply disappeared.

10. And what about the WEK? Is this just a build on an existing successful urban legend formula or, do the WEK represent something more sinister, powerful and diabolical?

I can offer you no definitive answers. I will continue to research this phenomenon, as it is fascinating. I think I have made my own theory quite clear. I believe the BEK to be demonic soul eaters and I believe them to be extremely dangerous.

The next time there is a knock at your door, will you answer it with trepidation? Just bear this in mind however. There are those who believe that once you know and have heard about the BEK, you will have an encounter with them. Good luck!

Finally, here is one more encounter in which the demonic nature of the BEK is hinted at....

This happened to me a couple of years ago. I had just moved out of my parents' house and was living in a house in New Jersey. I was home one night watching TV and had the porch door open. It was getting later, and I kept thinking about closing it. I got up to close up the house for the night and my dog started growling, which turned into barking. He was going crazy at the porch door but wasn't going outside to investigate. I looked over and a boy was standing there. He was about twelve and didn't say anything. He just stood staring at me. I asked him who he was, and he didn't say anything. I asked again, and he just looked at me and asked to come in.

By this point I was absolutely terrified. I thought this boy was going to kill me — even though he was just a young kid. I couldn't see his eyes as it was dark, so I didn't think for a second there was any reason to be scared. It was when I turned on the light that I saw his eyes. They were totally black. I felt as though I had been hit in the stomach with a baseball bat. I felt completely winded. He asked to come in again. I told him he couldn't. He just stared at me. I was in pain by this point and could hardly stand. Then he was gone. I stood up, closed the door and never left it open again late at night.

This was not a person. It was a demon of some kind and I was so lucky to have survived. I felt the life being sucked from my body. I have never read about an experience like this before.

Submitted by Jake W.

Book Two - The Black-Eyed Demons Are Coming!

In my first book on the BEK (published above), I came to the conclusion that this phenomenon has been around for a lot longer than most people might believe, and that the Black-Eyed People may just be demons that feed upon the souls of humanity. Since publishing that book, many more people have related their experiences with Black Eyed People to us and there is nothing in any of their stories that has made me change my mind - nothing at all. In fact, the last encounter in this book suggests that is indeed their true nature.

The Black-Eyed People encounter stories have been labeled a modern urban legend, yet I found evidence to suggest that black-eyed people have been with us for millennia in various guises as humanity's bogeymen. These people largely exist in the shadows of our subconscious and yet, from time-to-time, they emerge into daylight. Is it our fear of the unknown, the darkness that exists on the edge of sleep or death populated by monsters and demons that haunts us so?

A recently submitted experience sent in to us suggests that this might well be so.

> *This took place several years ago when I was staying with a friend of mine, and her family in Maine. Her parents had a summer place out there and I would go there with them quite often.*
>
> *We were in my friend's bedroom when I saw something walk past the window. This was a second-floor bedroom, so I was quite shocked to see something go past a window so high up. I didn't get much of a look at it — but I know it was completely white - pale even.*

After that, I tried to tell myself I hadn't seen anything. My friend didn't seem to be bothered by it so we both spent the afternoon reading and talking together.

The next day we were outside, and I had forgotten about the bedroom incident. We were in the garden when I quite felt strange – sick to my stomach. I wanted to go inside straight away. My friend wanted to stay outside, but she gave in, and we went back to her bedroom. I was looking out of the window when I saw him. There was a man standing in the garden wearing all black and a black hat, looking up at me in the bedroom. He waved at me and I saw his eyes. They were completely black. After the wave, he lifted the hat off of his head and beckoned me to come to him. I stood completely still and did nothing.

He stood there for a few seconds and then just faded away, still smiling. I didn't see him again – but I knew he was bad news. The way he waved at me was creepy.

A few years later I asked my friend about that incident and she didn't seem to remember anything about it. She said that she had never seen any such man in that area. Their neighbors were all families. There were few older people in the area. I have no idea who he was, or what he wanted.

Submitted by Louise Stillman, Florida

This is the stuff of nightmares. Unknown people dressed all in black with black eyes, beckoning to us from a distance. What did Louise actually see? What did the man want? And why did he have black eyes?

Commonly, nightmares are more terrifying because they happen in broad daylight with people all around and yet no one else seems to notice. The object of the nightmare in seen only by us, and everyone else carries on, oblivious to our increasing sense of horror. Like in this recent account.

> *A few weeks ago, I was walking down my street to get my car out of the garage when I noticed a homeless man sitting on a bench-like thing outside the garage. I had never seen him before, as he wasn't a regular on that block. There are few homeless people in my area — so he was very noticeable. As I passed by, he looked up at me and caught my eye.*

> *"Please spare some change. Anything you can spare will help me." He said.*

> *I was thinking about offering him some change, but then realized that all I had was some change buried in my handbag somewhere. I kept walking, pretending not to hear the man. I felt a pang of remorse as I passed him but continued. He continued to beg, and then as I sauntered away from him, he said,*

> *"Please spare some change. Please Michaela."*

> *I turned around as most people would hearing their name called, and I was met with this homeless man's strange, sinister stare. I was shocked that the man knew my name, being that I was not wearing anything that would identify me,*

and that I had never met him before. There was no logical explanation for him knowing it.

When I looked back at him, I saw that his eyes were black, bottomless, and almost hypnotic. There was absolutely no white in his eyes. His stare was truly frightening. It was evil, but it was powerful, and I felt as though I had hands running up and down my back. I truly felt that that he was not a person. It was a creature — and it knew everything about me.

It continued to stare at me and he stopped begging as other people passed by. I was so unbelievably frightened and speechless. I have no idea what it was or who it was, and why it called my name. I have never seen that man again on the street, and I don't ever want to.

Submitted by Michaela Jackson

It is broad daylight and seemingly just an innocent encounter with a homeless person. However, the experience takes on a different order of menace altogether when her name is used by this total stranger who also has pitch black eyes. It is a nightmarish experience. Notice also the fear and sense of evil when the black eyes are revealed. This powerful and irrational fear is a key component of all Black-Eyed people encounters.

Here is another encounter that took place in broad daylight by a park full of people eating their lunches and enjoying moments there.

This happened on October 19, 2006 at around 1pm or so. I usually parked my car at a park for my lunch, as a lot of people did that day. I had parked on a side of the park where there were no cars near me - only a truck facing my car from the opposite side. I had an uneasy feeling about the truck and had to move the car to another spot.

As I sat in my car eating lunch, a man walks past my car toward the pond/path. Then he appears near the front my car hood. I said to myself,

"Oh, what an ugly/odd looking person,"

It seemed as if he could read my mind, as he turned to glare at me with sinister look. His eyes were all black. I thought I was seeing things.

I had to go back to work then. On the way back, a utility truck backed into my car and I was wrecked. I never went back to that area again.

Submitted by Patti

Notice how the encounter is linked with bad luck just moments after as she has an accident and her car is wrecked.

The nightmarish quality that goes with encounters with these Black-Eyed folks is magnified when it involves Black Eyed kids (BEK). These pale-faced, black-eyed kids are often described as robotic, emotionless, and insistent. They always want to be let in.

The next encounter is a good example and has many aspects of the typical BEK encounter of the modern urban legend. There is just one problem – this story and encounter takes place long before the modern urban legend took off.

I was around twelve when this incident took place. I didn't know anything about Black Eyed kids until a few years ago when I started reading reports on the Internet about these strange people. My story is a little different to those other accounts.

I was sitting in my Mom's car waiting for her to return. She was inside Wal-Mart and I had elected to wait in the car with my book. A young boy had walked past the car a few times – and I hadn't really taken that much notice of him. The fourth or fifth time the boy went past, I think he noticed me as he came over to the car and stared in at me. I tried to ignore him and read my book – but he started whispering.

"Let me in",

I knew the front doors were locked and I quickly checked the doors at the back. My side was unlocked, but the side the boy was on was locked. I locked my side. The boy kept pleading to be left in. He then went quiet and stared at me for a few minutes before walking away.

I want to talk about the eyes. This boy had completely black eyes. There was no other color to be seen. Just pure blackness. He didn't blink. He didn't wince or show any emotion. His face was stony white. When he spoke, I seemed to hear the words in my head more than through my ears. When he tapped on the window it was slow and methodical. He did not seem to be in any danger or need my help. He was not panicking. It was almost like he was a robot under the control of someone, or something, else.

The weirdest thing about this encounter was that

my Mother returned to the car a few minutes later and complained that some woman had approached her and had asked for the keys to her car. She said my Mother had blocked her in and this woman want wanted to move her car. My Mom knew she hadn't. This strange woman then became quite insistent and my Mother was forced to ask a security guard to help her. To my knowledge our incidents had taken place at exactly the same time. She also told me that the woman's eyes were strange... Not completely black - but almost.

Submitted by Yanni Imbrugen

So, were these two incidents related? I think so. But how did two seemingly unconnected people manage to communicate so effectively over such a distance? Keep in mind that this happened in the 1970's before the micro-technology of today. Were they under the control of another person, or were they able to communicate telepathically? What is going on?

The scene seems even more terrifying as it takes place in the parking lot of Wal-Mart surrounded by people and traffic. It's as if they walk among us, beside us, even waiting for their moment to approach us, and for our own personal nightmare to begin. That moment can occur at any time and in any context. Imagine setting off for a routine showing of real estate only to find that today was your turn to meet them?

Of course, most BEK stories take place at night, or more accurately, in the early hours when small children should be at home and in bed sleeping. Things take on an even more sinister and frightening aspect after dark when no one is around, and we are alone in near silence.

The typical BEK story is the one in which a quiet knock disturbs the peace of the night. A young child or children are on the doorstep and their very presence causes an unexplained fear. They ask to come in, to enter. They look vulnerable and alone, and the conflict between the need to care for a young child and the rising fear that you are feeling is difficult to handle. Until that is, you see the black soulless eyes staring at you and then that fear finds its fury as you slam the door and retreat into the safety of your own home. Like in this encounter.

I usually go to sleep late at night, spending time reading books, watching TV, or listening to music. A few nights ago, after listening to music for a long time, I became sleepy, and removed my headphones. I clearly remember checking the time and it was around 3 a.m. I was simply lying down trying to sleep and that's when I heard a sound. Concentrating further, I realized that it was a knocking sound and probably made by a little child. As gentle as it was, it seemed to reverberate through the house as though it were coming through a giant speaker.

I checked the other rooms in our house, and my family was all sound asleep. I also checked the neighborhood for lights, and I couldn't find any. I was really confused and went to the dining room from where the sound was loudest.

I noticed that the sound was coming from outside. I went to the door and I could see the shape of a small child standing outside on our porch. I felt sick. I opened the door and a small child stood there. I turned on the porch lights and I could see that he was dressed in black. I asked him what he wanted, and he just stared at me.

He had completely black eyes.

I closed the door and the knocking started again. I

became really confused this time and went to my room. As soon as I entered my room, the knocking sound stopped abruptly. I decided to let it go and get some sleep. I closed my door and climbed into my bed when I heard a hard knock on my bedroom door. At the same time, there was a loud thud on my window. This thud made the glass rattle and shake. I thought the window was going to break. Somehow – and I don't know how, I fell asleep. I have no idea how that happened. I just remember the window shaking and then waking up the following morning.

When I woke up in the morning, I tried to dismiss the experiences as my imagination. When I told my Dad about this, he asked me to lock my door at night and to get to sleep earlier.

I thought it was all over, but from that day, I feel a presence with me in my room every night. It never tried to communicate with me or scare me, but I could always feel it with me at night when I'm alone in my room.

Submitted by Sheila Canavero

This experience left Sheila with a lasting presence. A fear that would not go away and one wonders if, in fact, she actually did let them in and simply does not remember doing so? There is no doubt a number of forces are at work when the BEK call and despite the fear, and the feeling of great danger, the hypnotic effect of the quiet compelling voice can cause people to do things that perhaps they otherwise would not do.

Those who have an encounter with the BEK often remark on their strange behavior and language. They do not act as small children might. They use old-fashioned words and language and are often dressed strangely. They may have well stepped out of another era or dimension or, as I have said above, from the edge of our reality. Their very presence strikes an irrational fear reaction. A terrifying fear of losing one's humanity, or indeed, our soul.

There is also a hint of the ill effects of the encounter in terms of headaches and so on. However, it is what appears to be an ability to see the future on the part of the BEK that is really creepy.

This took place in Arizona in the mid-1980's. One late evening, I woke up to loud knocks on the front door of my house. My husband was fast asleep, and I didn't want to go down and open the door. It wasn't normal for us to have late night visitors — so I did wonder if it was an accident of some type? I looked out of the window and I couldn't see anything. It was pitch black outside. I woke my husband and asked him to go down and find out what was happening. He wasn't very happy — but got up, put his robe on and went downstairs.

I watched from the landing as he opened the door. Two children were standing there. Both looked young, and both looked like they were frozen. I know there was a boy and a girl. My husband asked them if they had been in an accident. They nodded. He asked them if their parents were with them. They shook their heads.

"Our parents are coming for us," one of them said.

My husband was still half-asleep and started closing the door.

"Let us in", one of them said. "Let us in."

I watched as my husband opened the door and they walked in. He was obviously not in control of his own body. He doesn't take orders — but he did that night. I could see that both the children looked like they were eight years old. I went downstairs and asked them if they would like to sit down. We went through to the kitchen and they sat. Our dog went crazy. I had to shut him in another room. He would not stop barking. Looking back now he knew what these "kids" were.

I tried to make small talk with the kids. But they didn't say anything. My husband said nothing. It was then that he started to complain about stomach pains. He said that he felt as though he had been "stuck with a sword." I tried to help him, the kids didn't move. I left the room — and when I came back my husband had passed out, and the kids couldn't be found. I called 911 and asked for an ambulance.

I didn't even think about the kids until the next day. My husband was taken to hospital and needed to have immediate surgery to remove his appendix. The doctors said that he had a rumbling appendix and would have died if he had ignored it. The thing is he had never had any issue with his appendix before that night.

Who were those kids? Why did they want to hurt us? I know that they caused my husband's issues, and I want to know why.

Cyndi Mankowitz, Arizona

That encounter is unusual for not many stories of the BEK include them being allowed inside the home. The one or two stories of encounters in which people let the BEK in did not end well as I wrote in my previous BEK book and, neither did this one. The husband got sick and he got sick immediately. And, what happened to those kids?

The next encounter is actually quite exciting in terms of the Black-Eyed People. Firstly, it is set in the 1950's - long before the supposed beginning of BEK encounters in the US and secondly, it happened in the UK. This sort of encounter tells us much about the phenomenon.

My late father-in-law told me about his incident with a black-eyed person. He was living in Nottingham, United Kingdom, at the time.

One night when everyone in the house was asleep, my father heard a knock on the door and went to see who was there. He looked through the window and what he saw there sent shivers up his spine. There was a dark figure standing in front of the door and he saw that it had no face. Looking at it was like looking into a pitch-black hole. My father could not move and stood very still, not knowing what to do.

The figure knocked several times and my father eventually answered the door. He opened it slowly and to his surprise saw a man with a pale white face standing there. The man said nothing. He didn't even make a movement. It was my father who noticed his eyes. As soon as he had seen the eyes the figure disappeared. My father looked out of the window after recovering from shock and saw it standing underneath the streetlight. It stood there for a few minutes and then vanished into thin air.

This incident would have taken place in the 1950's. My father worked in England for ten years and never had another occurrence like it. Has anyone else heard of this disappearing figure with black eyes?

Submitted by Enoch Kennedy, Florida

In this instance, it's not a child but a man, however the effects are the same. It is a nightmare scenario in which fear reaches a crescendo and one fears for one's soul.

The problem with nightmares is that we can sometimes black them out completely. Forget them and deny that they ever occurred at all. It is best that way sometimes. Is that what happened to Matteo?

It was about 10pm in late June when this happened, and it really creeped me out.

I live in Colombia in the countryside. I was forced one day to move my PC to our third-Floor studio to get a better signal from the modem in our house. While I was setting up the PC, I noticed that my I Phone's iCloud Storage was so large that it could not actually complete a backup. This made me spend the next half an hour clearing my phone of old junk I no longer used. Lastly, I began to erase old pictures that I didn't wish to keep anymore.

I cleared almost all of the photos leaving just the oldest ones. There in the top row next to the very first photograph that I took with the phone of my dogs, was a really very creepy photo of a kid with black eyes just staring into the camera. It was a very disturbing image.

I have no idea where this picture came from! It was very old, and I think I would have noticed it earlier, but the photo seemed to have appeared from nowhere.

I tried tapping on the photo to enlarge it and to get a better look at it to see if I could discern anything else, but instead, the photo app crashed. When I went back after the crash, the picture was gone, while every other picture was still there. I still have absolutely no idea where it came from.

I didn't take the photo. I don't know anyone who would send me such a picture.

This is not made up. It really happened, and it scared me to death. I spent the next hour and a half looking for any possible answer. I often think about finding that photo on my phone.

I learnt about the BEK a few years ago through some of those odd conspiracy TV shows that sometimes pop up in Discovery Chanel and such, but I was never really convinced about it until that picture just popped up without any reasonable explanation.

How did the photo get there? It makes me shudder to think about it.

Submitted by Matteo S.

The question remains – what are these black-eyed creatures and what do they want? Are they really demons that walk among us? Legends and myths are full of them. They occupy the dark forests, lonely, and desolate places waiting to steal our souls. They occupy the far recesses of our minds where they haunt our nightmares and imaginations creating fear. Perhaps it is that they feed on? Or, perhaps, they really are seeking souls...

I've read a lot of your stories about Black-Eyed people and would like to share an experience my brother had some years ago, in Nashville. This is a true story he related to me one night over a beer. My brother is an extremely serious man and I wouldn't bet against his word.

The story my brother shared with me was about extremely strange, evil, and clairvoyant black-eyed man that he and his friends encountered a few years back in Nashville, TN.

My brother and his buddies were having dinner at a restaurant when a strange man walked into the restaurant and made for their table. At first my brother just thought he was a friendly drunk. He kept his head down, walked erratically and seemed to have no concept of there being other people in the restaurant. This man sat down at their table and tried to make as though he knew what they were talking about. But it was strange – he laughed at all the wrong things and talked over other people. He seemed to have no concept at all about people.

His appearance was more of a nuisance than anything else at this point, and none of the guys seemed interested in talking to this stranger, but he managed to make his way into their circle. The man seemed to want to just melt into the group. He kept looking towards the door as though he expected someone to come in after him.

My brother said that out of nowhere the mood of this stranger changed completely, and so did the subject matter, as he asked my brother's friend,

"If I could give you anything, what would it be?"

At first the friend laughed it off, but the stranger let it be known by his tone that he was completely serious, and he asked him again,

"If I could give you anything?"

The friend replied something like,

"I don't know, man.... Money and Lindsay Lohan as my girlfriend."

Well, things got weird when the stranger admitted how he could do these things for him in exchange for his soul. He then started openly sharing the details of his possession, and how it was his duty to find a human willing to sacrifice his soul, one person every year or something like that.

My brother noticed his eyes became blackened at some point, and the most indescribable evil aura was around him. The guys were all getting freaked out, yet still thought this guy was probably full of it. The stranger wanted to prove his ability, so he asked the guy to ask him any question about himself, and he could answer it. So, my brother's friend asked,

"Okay, what is my grandma's name?"

The demon man answered

"Megan Jane Hofstetter."

Which was, to their amazement, correct! At this point, things were getting strange and it was getting very late. My brother and his friends decided to get the hell out of there. The man didn't follow them, but they couldn't get him out of their heads that night. All of them dreamed about that man.

The next day they decided to head home and cut their journey short. What stands out most to my brother is the incredibly evil, creepy, strange feeling that he and his friends all witnessed and felt firsthand. I wanted to share this story as it fascinated me for years. The problem is it is very creepy to talk about, but I have this urge, I can't explain, to talk about it.

Submitted by James Deacon, TN

So, watch out! The Black-Eyed people are best left alone. Do not let them in for to do so is actually giving them permission to steal your soul. Remember this too. They say that once you know about them, you will encounter them. Just as Neil did...

This took place one summer several years ago. We were in the back yard. My mother was sitting in a chair to my left and dad was sitting to the right, I was in the middle with my favorite blanket. It was a mild day, extremely pleasant– until I looked at the power line running across the backyard.

Now on this power line was a tall man walking in black. The one thing that makes me remember this is the eyes. They were completely black. That feeling when he looked at me though just terrified me. I blinked, and he was gone. Nobody else saw him. It was one of the most terrifying things that has ever happened to me. He was standing still on the powerline, he didn't move, he didn't smile. He was just standing there looking at me.

I tried to tell my parents about him — but they thought I was imagining things. In fact, my dad accused me of trying to spoil the day. Mom would listen, but she didn't believe me. I spent that whole day wondering who it was, and why he was on the powerlines looking down at me.

Now I have not seen this thing again since that time, but I have experienced quite a bit of weird things. Every time I think about this, I can see the eyes perfectly like the first time in my mind staring at me.

Neil Shannon, Texas

Neil's story is one that is shared by many people who see Black Eyed people that no one else can. There are several such encounters in this book. Is Neil dreaming? Is he seeing things? Certainly, he appears to be experiencing a waking nightmare and it is this very quality that evokes such fear. In the next encounter, a Black-Eyed man appears in a garden turning a woman's day into a nightmare.

It was June 2016, Roseville California, 3pm. I began to make my way to my ex-sister-in-law's house. Four of my nieces stay with her and her new husband. I knocked on the door to smiling faces and a barking dog. This dog wouldn't stop barking and stayed close to the two littlest girls, 3 and 4 years old. Their names, Devin and Danni, golden hair and blue eyes. Their mother, Lindsey was finishing dinner before heading out to get the other two older girls, Ashlynn and Harley, 10 years old and 15 years old. Lindsey asked me to watch the two little ones while she ran to get the other girls.

I sat on the couch with Danni and Devin, but then Devin ran to the back-sliding door and screamed. Danni ran over, held her sister and screamed. I jumped up as fast as I could. Behind Danni, I saw a shadow disappear into nothing in the backyard. The dog was barking, and the girls kept screaming then dashed down the hallway as their mother and older sisters walked into the front door. The dog didn't move at all but glared out the slider door. For a moment, I completely forgot there was a shadow in the backyard during complete daylight.

It was now 3:30pm and everyone either doing homework or eating. Lindsey and I were having amazing afternoon together. It was fine until she walked to the slider door and looked out for a moment before she slowly closed the curtain. The two little ones point out the door yelling "MOMMY, THERE IS A MAN OUT THERE" over and over. Lindsey took a long time closing the curtain and as I got close, she yelled at the girls "ENOUGH ALREADY THERE IS NO ONE OUT

THERE." However, before she could close the curtain fully, I saw a man standing in the back yard, slim man, dark eyes, suit black, white shirt, skinny thin black tie, he was pale white, his lips very light pink, and a black hat like a detective's hat. He tilted his head to his right and held up his left hand, pushing his index finger to his lips, saying "SHHHHH" as his head turned back right side up. It felt like doom was near, felt like there was anger in that house, and all I wanted to do was run away. I went to the garage to have a cig. I couldn't believe what I had seen and then Lindsey came out. She told me that I was unwelcome in her home and I was never to see her kids again. The anger in her eyes. I watched them turn into darker color – into black.

I left that day, depressed, sad, and felt something like death enter my soul. To this day that memory scares me, I still hear him speak in my head, I wasn't supposed to see him, he wanted me to stay "AHHH ", that was the only noise my ears heard. Though my minds kept hearing, YOU SHOULDN'T ABLE TO SEE ME.

What made me really scared was that three months before that slim man entered my mind or my mind made it up because of the fear, I am not sure. I heard a podcast on the radio going on about black eyed children and adults. I went home after Lindsey yelling at me, saying I was unwanted. I told my husband, and he said "YOU ARE NOT ALONE. ONCE YOU HEAR ABOUT THEM OR SEE THEM OR BOTH, THEY ARE WITH YOU FOR LIFE." My husband doesn't recall saying that at all but remembers researching the slim man and telling me facts. Today, April 2017, I heard about the black-eyed children again, then I knew I had to say something because I wasn't alone, and I want answers.

Submitted by Michelle Bair

Here is another experience in which the Black-Eyed person creates fear and confusion in a woman. While she sits in fear, her friend apparently sees nothing. So, is this a figment of her imagination or do Black eyed people appear selectively?

I hadn't heard of the BEK until recently, I also came across reports of BEK adults – this happened in 1976 when I was 18yrs., back then I was confident, fun loving and didn't scare easily

My friend and I decided on a weeks' holiday in London, we had saved for months as had intended on going to a show, nightclubs and buying fashionable clothes, we were on our way to do the latter when this happened-

We excitedly clambered on to the tube looking forward to hitting the fashionable boutiques, took our seats chattering about shoes, dresses etc. I happened to look up and on the next section of seats, facing me was a thin man with a long face, he had black hair, pale waxy skin and small black eyes. He sat impassively staring at me with no expression whatsoever, I felt a thud of panic which grew into complete terror and regardless of the amount of people on that tube I had the feeling of being completely alone and in terrible danger. I tried telling my friend who was oblivious, and she kept saying 'where, where, I don't see him?'

What?! You can't see him? You can't bloody miss him! – I wanted to scream but for some odd reason I felt I had to keep quiet and avoid his gaze. I don't know how I managed that short journey. I dragged my friend off the tube and made a rush to the lift in a blind panic, I would be safe when out of the Underground and in the daylight. Huddled in the busy lift praying the doors would close I almost collapsed in terror when there he was in the lift also, no emotion, black eyes watching me – I turned and whimpered to my friend that he was standing in the corner, she said there was nobody with that description there. I kept my head bowed, there was an air of menace and nobody was aware of it. I pushed my way out when the lift doors opened, then turned to check where he was – he didn't come out the lift, there was only the 1 floor ... he had vanished!

What puzzles me is why didn't my friend see him, why was she so oblivious to my distress, she knew I wasn't an irrational person, when I tried to explain she said she couldn't remember me speaking!? It was as though I was in a bubble with that man and anyone outside of it was unaware of the great threat and danger ... It was awful – who was he?

Submitted by Elizabeth Mac

What about being stalked by a BEK?

Working the night shift for a data center in Ohio had a creepy exchange and posted his tale anonymously as Noetic. It was around 5 am on July 31, 2010. Noetic was taking a smoke break outside when he noticed two teenage boys standing motionlessly and staring at him from across the street. Immediately feeling unnerved, he snubbed out his smoke and went back inside.

No more than ten minutes later, the intercom buzzed. Noetic checked the monitors and there they were. The two boys had made their way over to his building and were now staring into the surveillance camera like they could see him through it. Through the speaker he asked what they wanted. They said nothing but motioned for him to come outside. He hit the speaker button again and told them to go away. They didn't leave but continued to stare into the camera as if they were watching Noetic as he worked. Noetic was fed up after about 10 minutes of this creepfest, so he went to the door to chase them off.

Right before opening the door, he saw them through the one-way glass and was horrified to see their eyes were completely black. He knew he had to open up the door and tell them to get out, and he decided he'd call the police if he had to. As if the boy read his mind, the moment the door opened, he said, "That will not be necessary, sir, we simply need to use your phone, can you let us in?"

Noetic was not about to fall for that nonsense. He pulled out his cell and threatened to call the police if they didn't leave. He made sure the door was locked and he went back to the monitor. Only one boy was still there staring at the camera. Then he realized the second boy positioned himself out back and was staring into camera three. Noetic called the police. Both boys moved into a blind spot with *no camera coverage. Noetic waited for them to reappear but they simply vanished. The police arrived around 6:00 am, and both boys were gone.*

The next story is truly terrifying and results in a fatality. Is that what the BEK wanted?

Heading to his car on the third floor of a parking garage when one of the guys from the conference he'd just attended, Doug, asked him to drive him around the block a few times. He said there were some freaky-looking kids hanging around his car and was hoping to kill some time while waiting for them to wander off. Jon let Doug in and they started cruising. When they neared his car, Jon saw the group Doug was talking about and agreed they were creepy.

Three kids, two boys and a girl, all gothed out. The girl looked about 15, the boys around 14 and 10. They were intense, but Jon described it as if he began itching behind his eyes and really needed to look at them. He stopped driving. The kids maneuvered around his car and the youngest one said, "It's scary out there all alone, and we just wanted a ride home."

Apparently, Doug had interacted with the younger one earlier and had agreed to drive him home, but the two older ones creeped him out and he changed his mind. Jon felt as if his heart was going to erupt from his throat as adrenaline raced through him. Doug said he was getting out of the car. As soon as he reached for the handle, it was like the children got older somehow, and he saw their eyes were solid black - no pupil, no iris, nothing. Just black. Jon threw the car into reverse and squealed the car backwards about 60 feet.

The kids began to pursue them, Jon took the car around the lot's corners going around 30 miles per hour. He felt that they would die if he let those kids get in the car. He sped down three floors only to find the oldest boy was already at the bottom of the garage when they came out. They sped past him out of the garage and when Jon glanced in his rearview, the boy was gone and so was that menacing feeling that had been building inside him since making contact with those kids.

They waited a few minutes before going back and Doug was able to get in his car and head home. The black-eyed children were nowhere in sight. Upon leaving the garage for the second time that night, the menacing feeling returned. Jon was behind Doug's car watching helplessly as it misjudged the time it would take to get through the intersection on a yellow light. Doug was struck by a truck and died instantly. Jon saw the three black-eyed children still lurking about two blocks away.

Here is a recent account submitted to us in which someone or something intervenes.

So, I was home alone one night just casually watching TV around 3AM when I heard a knock at my door. It's pretty late in the night, but my sister would pop in around this time unexpected all the time, but as I reached the door, I noticed it was increasingly quiet regardless that I live in the country, I didn't even hear crickets chirping outside.

When I opened the door there was a little boy staring at the ground wearing old-time like clothes possibly from the 70? He asked if he could come inside to use the bathroom. I thought this was strange because it's 3 in the morning. I ask the boy if he was lost or lived somewhere in town. He didn't answer but instead just said he really had to go if he could please come inside. As he looked up, I saw his pitch-black eyes. As I looked in his eyes, I heard a voice say loudly right beside me CLOSE THE DOOR NOW. I immediately slammed the door and looked beside me to see my uncle who passed away when I was a kid standing beside me. As I stood completely frozen, he spoke softly "I will always protect you and pointed to the necklace he gave me when he passed away. When I looked up, he was gone.

I looked out the window at the porch to see the kid, but he was gone. I locked the door and didn't open it until morning. I believe my uncle is my guardian angel. And I believe he saved me that night.

Submitted by Ezra to Weird Darkness and My Haunted Life Too

Finally, here is another tale involving BEK in which there are power outages and the BEK remain undetected by security cameras.

A gas station attendant in northeast Louisiana had

a terrifying encounter on November 2012. The gas station was creepy enough to begin with at 3am, but then the power went out. Led by the light of his cell phone, the attendant was able to get the generators going but the backup lighting was dim and only lit up certain areas, like the cash area and the parking lot, while the rest of the isolated establishment was cloaked in black. Out in that darkness he noticed movement: three children on bikes were heading his way.

They stood at the door and stared at the attendant. He felt creeped out, but they were just kids and it was way too late for them to be out. He opened the door and asked if they were okay. The young girl asked to use a phone, but as he handed his cell over to her, he realized her eyes were all black. "No, I need the real one!" She pointed at the landline inside. The thought of letting her inside sent chills up his spine. He shouted at all of them to leave as he slammed and locked the door.

The children stood there a bit longer, silently staring at him through the glass with their solid black eyes. Then they got back on their bikes and disappeared back into the darkness. The next morning, the attendant was eager to go through the surveillance footage. Unfortunately, the power outage cut the cameras off and they didn't boot back up with the generator. He had nothing to prove the events of the night before took place.

The stories continue to pour in. Each has its common and now expected themes of terror, black eyes, feelings of impending doom and so on but each is also different in terms of context. What are the Black-Eyed people? Are they demons as I postulated in my first exploration on the topic or are they simply an urban legend?

Let me know.

If you do, be sure to let us have the story of the encounter at www.myhauntedlifetoo.com

About G. Michael Vasey

G. Michael Vasey is a Yorkshire man and rabid Tigers (Hull City AFC) fan that has spent most of his adult life lost deep in Texas and more lately, in the Czech Republic. While lucky enough to write for a living as a leading analyst in the commodity trading and risk management industry, he surreptitiously writes strange poems and equally strange books and stories on the topics of metaphysics, occult and the paranormal on the side, hoping that one-day, someone might actually buy them.

After growing up experiencing ghosts, poltergeist and other strange and scary experiences, he developed an interest in magic and the esoteric. These days he fancies himself as a bit of a mystic and a magician to boot. Most of his inspiration for his scribbling comes from either meditation or occasionally, very loud heavy metal music.

He has appeared on radio shows such as Everyday Connection and X Radio with Rob McConnell to tell strange and scary stories. He has also been featured in Chat - Its Fate magazine and interviewed by Ghost Village and Novel Ideas amongst others.

He blogs addictively at www.garymvasey.com and he tweets micro thoughts at @gmvasey. He also reviews a lot of very weird books at www.strangebookreviews.com and collects true stories of the paranormal at www.yourhauntedlifetoo.com.

Do come over to My Haunted Life Too for a new true story every day.

Other Books

- **True Tales of Haunted Places** (Kindle)
- **The Most Haunted Country in the World – The Czech Republic** (Kindle and paperback)
- **Your Haunted Lives – Revisited** (Kindle and Audio book)
- **The Pink Bus** (Kindle and audio book)
- **Ghosts in The Machines** *(Kindle and audio book)*

- **How to Create Your Own Reality** *(Paperback and Kindle)*
- **God's Pretenders – Incredible Tales of Magic and Alchemy** *(Kindle and audio book)*
- **My Haunted Life – Extreme Edition** *(Paperback, audiobook and Kindle)*
- **My Haunted Life 3** *(Kindle, audiobook and eBook)*
- **My Haunted Life Too** *(Audio book, Kindle and eBook)*
- **My Haunted Life** *(Kindle, eBook and forthcoming audiobook)*
- **The Last Observer** *(Paperback, eBook and **Kindle**)*
- **The Mystical Hexagram** *(Paperback and Kindle)*
- **Inner Journeys – Explorations of the Soul** *(Paperback and Kindle)*

Other Poetry Collections

- **Death on The Beach** *(Kindle)*
- **The Art of Science** *(Paperback and Kindle)*
- **Best Laid Plans and Other Strange Tails** *(Paperback and Kindle)*
- **Moon Whispers** *(Paperback and Kindle)*
- **Astral Messages** *(Paperback and Kindle)*
- **Poems for the Little Room** *(Paperback and Kindle)*
- **Weird Tales** *(Paperback and Kindle)*

All of G. Michael's Vasey's books can be obtained on any Amazon site and some can be found on other book sites such as Barnes & Noble, Apple and more…. He offers signed and dedicated paperbacks from his website at http://www.garymvasey.com

Made in the USA
Coppell, TX
20 April 2021

54093842R00059